Minding you

taking care of the things that need to be taken care of. It also means taking care of the person that's taking care of all of those things. To be effective, we have to be mindful. When I say "Mind your business," I am saying, "take care of your business, and that begins with taking care of you. Enjoy this journal, as it is meant to help you mind your business.

How will you mind your business today? List 2 things: Take a walk, clean your desk...

Gratitude can help you be mindful. What are you grateful for today?

Tell yourself why you deserve grace today!

Look at what you have accomplished. Take a break and draw a funny picture.

Breathe In for 4 seconds

Hold your breath for 4 seconds

Exhale for 4 seconds

Who needs your understanding today and why?

What did you enjoy about today, this week, or this month?

Use all of the resources you have today to be more effective.

*If you just have to curse,
do it here first!*

What personal business have you been neglecting?

Personal business I've been neglecting:

Dates to get it done:

Do you feel like you've lost? What did you learn, today, this week this month this quarter? You didn't lose, you learned!

Help yourself and your team with self-care today?

Manage your emotions, just for the moment.

What top 3 things need your attention right now?

*Time for a mental break, so
you don't have a mental break!*

Give empathy, but not to the point of toxicity!

Retain, Remain, Release!

What will you retain from this journ(ey)al?

What will remain?

What will you release?